To Mum & Dad,
Lee, Terri & Steve

Text by Nicky Farthing
Illustrations copyright © 2000 Bernice Lum
This edition copyright © 2001 Lion Publishing

The moral rights of the author and illustrator
have been asserted

Published by
Lion Publishing
4050 Lee Vance View, Colorado Springs
CO 80918, USA
ISBN 0 7459 4501 5

First UK edition 2000
First US edition 2001
1 3 5 7 9 10 8 6 4 2 0

Library of Congress CIP data applied for

Typeset in 24/26 Kidprint MT
Printed and bound in Malaysia

**This Bible tale is adapted from the story of David and Goliath,
which can be found in 1 Samuel, chapter 17.**

The Knock-out Story of David & Goliath

Retold by Nicky Farthing
Illustrated by Bernice Lum

LION
Children's Books

All the animals were gloomy.
'Fierce soldiers have come to take our
land, our home,' announced King Hippo.
'Will anyone dare to fight them?'

The animals looked towards the army.

Then came a great shout.

I am
GOLIATH.
Who will dare
to fight me?

Out went David.

Big bully!
The Maker of the Jungle
will help me beat you.

Goliath was very angry.
And he began to run towards David.

David reached for a stone.

The fierce animals all ran away
with their tails between their legs.

David was carried high through the crowds. 'The Maker of the Jungle did help him!' all the animals cheered.